RACHEL

Never Alone

remembering God is with me

BIBLE READING PLAN
& JOURNAL

NEVER ALONE
Bible Reading Plan and Journal
PUBLISHED BY RACHEL WOJO
Copyright © 2017 by Rachel Wojnarowski

Visit **www.rachelwojo.com/shop**

Requests for information should be addressed to rachel@rachelwojo.com

Trade Paperback ISBN-13: 978-0692882047 (Rachel Wojo LLC)

ISBN-10: 0692882049

Cover design by Rachel Wojnarowski

Photo credit: Bigstock.com

Library of Congress Cataloging-in-Publication Data

Printed in the United States of America
2017—Second Edition--1002

Table of Contents

Table of Contents

A Personal Note from Rachel

❧❦❧❦❧❦❧

Dear Friend,

Thank you for joining in this Bible reading plan and journal for the reminder that God is always with you. My goal through Bible reading is to saturate my mind with the truth of God's Word, and I want that for you too!

Through reading daily Bible passages, praying, and listening to God, we're going to nurture and grow our relationship with him. This Bible reading plan and journal is specifically focused on knowing that our Heavenly Father will never leave us alone.

Whether we simply fail to recognize God's presence or we're wrapped up in hurts or hindrances, this journal, through the Bible reading plan and journaling exercises, will realign our focus on God's promise to always be with us.

I.can't.wait!

Rachel

Remembering God is With me

Welcome to the Never Alone Bible Reading Plan & Journal. I'm so excited to begin this journey with you! For the next thirty-one days, we are going to dig into God's word and grow closer to Him. Together we'll make the choice to remember that God is always with us and we are never alone.

> The situations we wish God would remove from our lives are often the lessons God uses to teach us to rely on him.
> --*One More Step*

Are you ready to learn to believe God is always with you? You can share what you are learning on social media by using the hashtags #neveralonejournal and #biblereadingplan or you can just keep it between you and God.

4 Simple Steps
to growing in faith

step 1:

Pray: Spend some time with God in prayer.
Prayer is simply having a conversation with

step 2:

Read the Bible passage for the day one time
slowly, soaking in each phrase. Read again if

step 3:

Answer the daily question.

step 4:

Complete the journaling section.

Praying God's Promises

God's Word is full of promises to believers. According to BibleInfo.com, it has been estimated that there are 3573 promises in the Bible and other sources have cited as many as 7000!

Throughout Scripture, God promises that he is with us and he will never leave us. Not only are we the benefactors of his promises, the power of praying God's promises to him is immeasurable. This Bible reading plan and journal includes a section on praying God's promises back to him. Each day's reading offers a fill-in-the-blank journaling section to help you restate God's promises. You can use the example below to help you get started. Enjoy!

Praying the Promise Example

Dear God,

Thank you for being ___with me___.

Please forgive me for ___failing to remember this___.

Help me to recognize your presence in my life.

Your Word says you will never leave me.

and I believe it. Please give me strength and wisdom.

Show me how to live this promise today.

I praise You for the victory.

Amen.

Presence

God will never
abandon me.

What is one
statement of truth
from this passage that
reminds me I'm not
alone?

_____
_____
_____
_____
_____
_____
_____
_____
_____

Praying the Promise

Dear God,

Thank you for being _____.

Please forgive me for _____.

Help me to recognize_____.

Your Word says _____

and I believe it. Please give me _____.

Show me how to _____.

I praise You for the victory.

Amen.

When I begin to feel lonely, I will pray God's promises in one of the following ways:
(Check your focus.)

- o Thank God that He is always with me.
- o Tell Him I believe that He is listening.
- o Ask God to help me notice His grace in my daily life.
- o Request the wisdom to see opportunities to embrace relationship.

Pen A Prayer

_____

_____

_____

_____

_____

_____

_____

_____

Always

Jesus promises to
be with me
for eternity.

When I'm
experiencing
loneliness, what
promise from this
passage would refocus
my feelings?

_____
_____
_____
_____
_____
_____
_____
_____
_____
_____

Praying the Promise

Dear God,

Thank you for being _____.

Please forgive me for _____.

Help me to recognize_____.

Your Word says _____

and I believe it. Please give me _____.

Show me how to _____.

I praise You for the victory.

Amen.

When I begin to feel lonely, I will pray God's promises in one of the following ways:
(Check your focus.)

- o Thank God that He will never leave me.
- o Tell Hm that I want to sense His presence.
- o Invite Him to encourage my heart to share His love.
- o Ask the Lord to help me see that I am not alone.

Pen A Prayer

_____

_____

_____

_____

_____

_____

_____

_____

Isaiah 41:1-10

Personal

God says he
is my God.

When I'm
experiencing
loneliness, what
promise from this
passage would refocus
my feelings?

_____
_____
_____
_____
_____
_____
_____
_____
_____

Praying the Promise

Dear God,

Thank you for being _____.

Please forgive me for _____.

Help me to recognize_____.

Your Word says _____

and I believe it. Please give me _____.

Show me how to _____.

I praise You for the victory.

Amen.

When I begin to feel lonely, I will pray God's promises in one of the following ways:
(Check your focus.)

- o Thank God that He is always with me.
- o Tell Him I believe that He is listening.
- o Ask God to help me notice His grace in my daily life.
- o Request the wisdom to see opportunities to embrace relationship.

Pen A Prayer

_____

_____

_____

_____

_____

_____

_____

_____

How personal
will I
allow God
to be
in my life
today?

Joshua 1:1-9

Wherever

When I'm experiencing loneliness, what promise from this passage would refocus my feelings?

No matter my path, God is right there.

_____
_____
_____
_____
_____
_____
_____
_____

Praying the Promise

Dear God,

Thank you for being _____.

Please forgive me for _____.

Help me to recognize_____.

Your Word says _____

and I believe it. Please give me _____.

Show me how to _____.

I praise You for the victory.

Amen.

When I begin to feel lonely, I will pray God's promises in one of the following ways:
(Check your focus.)

- o Thank God that He will never leave me.
- o Tell Hm that I want to sense His presence.
- o Invite Him to encourage my heart to share His love.
- o Ask the Lord to help me see that I am not alone.

Pen A Prayer

_____

_____

_____

_____

_____

_____

_____

_____

Psalm 23:1-6

Day 5

No Fear

God is present in both the sunshine and the storms.

What is one statement of truth from this passage that reminds me I'm not alone?

_____
_____
_____
_____
_____
_____
_____
_____

Praying the Promise

Dear God,

Thank you for being _____.

Please forgive me for _____.

Help me to recognize_____.

Your Word says _____

and I believe it. Please give me _____.

Show me how to _____.

I praise You for the victory.

Amen.

When I begin to feel lonely, I will pray God's promises in one of the following ways:
(Check your focus.)

- ○ Thank God that He is always with me.
- ○ Tell Him I believe that He is listening.
- ○ Ask God to help me notice His grace in my daily life.
- ○ Request the wisdom to see opportunities to embrace relationship.

Pen A Prayer

_____

_____

_____

_____

_____

_____

_____

_____

Jeremiah 23:23-30

No Secrets

God is never
far away.

When I'm
experiencing
loneliness, what
promise from this
passage would refocus
my feelings?

_____
_____
_____
_____
_____
_____
_____
_____
_____

Praying the Promise

Dear God,

Thank you for being _____.

Please forgive me for _____.

Help me to recognize_____.

Your Word says _____

and I believe it. Please give me _____.

Show me how to _____.

I praise You for the victory.

Amen.

When I begin to feel lonely, I will pray God's promises in one of the following ways:
(Check your focus.)

o   Thank God that He will never leave me.
o   Tell Hm that I want to sense His presence.
o   Invite Him to encourage my heart to share His love.
o   Ask the Lord to help me see that I am not alone.

Pen A Prayer

_____

_____

_____

_____

_____

_____

_____

_____

Promise

Unite in prayer with others and enjoy His presence.

What is one statement of truth from this passage that reminds me I'm not alone?

_____
_____
_____
_____
_____
_____
_____
_____

Praying the Promise

Dear God,

Thank you for being _____.

Please forgive me for _____.

Help me to recognize_____.

Your Word says _____

and I believe it. Please give me _____.

Show me how to _____.

I praise You for the victory.

Amen.

When I begin to feel lonely, I will pray God's promises in one of the following ways:
(Check your focus.)

- o Thank God that He is always with me.
- o Tell Him I believe that He is listening.
- o Ask God to help me notice His grace in my daily life.
- o Request the wisdom to see opportunities to embrace relationship.

Pen A Prayer

_____

_____

_____

_____

_____

_____

_____

_____

Never

The Lord goes before me; he will never forsake me.

When I'm experiencing loneliness, what promise from this passage would refocus my feelings?

_____
_____
_____
_____
_____
_____
_____
_____

Praying the Promise

Dear God,

Thank you for being _____.

Please forgive me for _____.

Help me to recognize_____.

Your Word says _____

and I believe it. Please give me _____.

Show me how to _____.

I praise You for the victory.

Amen.

When I begin to feel lonely, I will pray God's promises in one of the following ways:
(Check your focus.)

o   Thank God that He will never leave me.
o   Tell Hm that I want to sense His presence.
o   Invite Him to encourage my heart to share His love.
o   Ask the Lord to help me see that I am not alone.

Pen A Prayer

_____
_____
_____
_____
_____
_____
_____
_____

Matthew 1:20-25

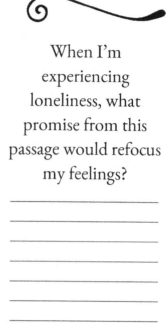

Day 9

Every Day

God woke me up this morning and his very breath gives me life.

When I'm experiencing loneliness, what promise from this passage would refocus my feelings?

_____
_____
_____
_____
_____
_____
_____
_____

Praying the Promise

Dear God,

Thank you for being _____.

Please forgive me for _____.

Help me to recognize_____.

Your Word says _____

and I believe it. Please give me _____.

Show me how to _____.

I praise You for the victory.

Amen.

When I begin to feel lonely, I will pray God's promises in one of the following ways:
(Check your focus.)

- o Thank God that He is always with me.
- o Tell Him I believe that He is listening.
- o Ask God to help me notice His grace in my daily life.
- o Request the wisdom to see opportunities to embrace relationship.

Pen A Prayer

_____

_____

_____

_____

_____

_____

_____

_____

The very name
of Jesus,
IMMANUEL,
means
God with us.

Without

Admitting my
need for God
is powerful.

What is one
statement of truth
from this passage that
reminds me I'm not
alone?

_____
_____
_____
_____
_____
_____
_____
_____

Praying the Promise

Dear God,

Thank you for being _____.

Please forgive me for _____.

Help me to recognize_____.

Your Word says _____

and I believe it. Please give me _____.

Show me how to _____.

I praise You for the victory.

Amen.

When I begin to feel lonely, I will pray God's promises in one of the following ways:
(Check your focus.)

o Thank God that He will never leave me.
o Tell Hm that I want to sense His presence.
o Invite Him to encourage my heart to share His love.
o Ask the Lord to help me see that I am not alone.

Pen A Prayer

_____
_____
_____
_____
_____
_____
_____
_____

Day 11

With

When I admit my need to God, he loves to hear me.

When I'm experiencing loneliness, what promise from this passage would refocus my feelings?

_____
_____
_____
_____
_____
_____
_____
_____
_____
_____

Praying the Promise

Dear God,

Thank you for being _____.

Please forgive me for _____.

Help me to recognize_____.

Your Word says _____

and I believe it. Please give me _____.

Show me how to _____.

I praise You for the victory.

Amen.

When I begin to feel lonely, I will pray God's promises in one of the following ways:
(Check your focus.)

- o Thank God that He is always with me.
- o Tell Him I believe that He is listening.
- o Ask God to help me notice His grace in my daily life.
- o Request the wisdom to see opportunities to embrace relationship.

Pen A Prayer

_____

_____

_____

_____

_____

_____

_____

_____

Psalm 73:21-28

near

No place is too
low for God to
see me.

When I'm
experiencing
loneliness, what
promise from this
passage would refocus
my feelings?

_____
_____
_____
_____
_____
_____
_____
_____
_____

Praying the Promise

Dear God,

Thank you for being _____.

Please forgive me for _____.

Help me to recognize_____.

Your Word says _____

and I believe it. Please give me _____.

Show me how to _____.

I praise You for the victory.

Amen.

When I begin to feel lonely, I will pray God's promises in one of the following ways:
(Check your focus.)

- ○ Thank God that He will never leave me.
- ○ Tell Hm that I want to sense His presence.
- ○ Invite Him to encourage my heart to share His love.
- ○ Ask the Lord to help me see that I am not alone.

Pen A Prayer

_____

_____

_____

_____

_____

_____

_____

_____

Deut. 2:1-7

Day 13

Through

My God knows
my path straight
through my
wilderness.

What is one
statement of truth
from this passage that
reminds me I'm not
alone?

_____
_____
_____
_____
_____
_____
_____
_____

Praying the Promise

Dear God,

Thank you for being _____.

Please forgive me for _____.

Help me to recognize_____.

Your Word says _____

and I believe it. Please give me _____.

Show me how to _____.

I praise You for the victory.

Amen.

When I begin to feel lonely, I will pray God's promises in one of the following ways:
(Check your focus.)

- o Thank God that He is always with me.
- o Tell Him I believe that He is listening.
- o Ask God to help me notice His grace in my daily life.
- o Request the wisdom to see opportunities to embrace relationship.

Pen A Prayer

_____

_____

_____

_____

_____

_____

_____

_____

There is another
side to my
wilderness.
I am only going
through it.
I am not
camping in the
wilderness
permanently.
I am not
settling.
I am prepared to
keep moving
because
my God is
WITH ME!

Judges 6:6-16   Day 14

miracle

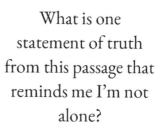

God is calling
me to be a
part of the
solution.

What is one
statement of truth
from this passage that
reminds me I'm not
alone?

_____
_____
_____
_____
_____
_____
_____
_____
_____

Praying the Promise

Dear God,
Thank you for being _____.
Please forgive me for _____.
Help me to recognize_____.
Your Word says _____
and I believe it. Please give me _____.
Show me how to _____.
I praise You for the victory.
Amen.

When I begin to feel lonely, I will pray God's promises in one of the following ways:
(Check your focus.)

o Thank God that He will never leave me.
o Tell Hm that I want to sense His presence.
o Invite Him to encourage my heart to share His love.
o Ask the Lord to help me see that I am not alone.

Pen A Prayer

_____
_____
_____
_____
_____
_____
_____
_____

Psalm 139:1-12

Light

There is no place I can go that God is not present.

What is one statement of truth from this passage that reminds me I'm not alone?

_____
_____
_____
_____
_____
_____
_____
_____

Praying the Promise

Dear God,

Thank you for being _____.

Please forgive me for _____.

Help me to recognize_____.

Your Word says _____

and I believe it. Please give me _____.

Show me how to _____.

I praise You for the victory.

Amen.

When I begin to feel lonely, I will pray God's promises in one of the following ways:
(Check your focus.)

- o Thank God that He is always with me.
- o Tell Him I believe that He is listening.
- o Ask God to help me notice His grace in my daily life.
- o Request the wisdom to see opportunities to embrace relationship.

Pen A Prayer

_____

_____

_____

_____

_____

_____

_____

_____

A Morning Prayer

Lord Jesus,
I praise you for the gift of another day-
For your mercies new each morning.
My eyes are open and my heart is beating;
Each of those mean you have a plan for me.
This minute. This hour. This day.
I don't know every step of your plan for today
But I know it will be for my good.
And I'm confident it will be for your glory.
Will you lead me, Jesus? I need you.
Will you order my steps, each one?
May your love flow through me
And may I embrace every opportunity
To share your love with others.
Amen

Psalm 139:13-24

Knitted

God knew me
even while I was
being created in
the womb.

When I'm
experiencing
loneliness, what
promise from this
passage would refocus
my feelings?

_____
_____
_____
_____
_____
_____
_____
_____
_____

Praying the Promise

Dear God,
Thank you for being _____.
Please forgive me for _____.
Help me to recognize_____.
Your Word says _____
and I believe it. Please give me _____.
Show me how to _____.
I praise You for the victory.
Amen.

When I begin to feel lonely, I will pray God's promises in one of the following ways:
(Check your focus.)

o   Thank God that He will never leave me.
o   Tell Hm that I want to sense His presence.
o   Invite Him to encourage my heart to share His love.
o   Ask the Lord to help me see that I am not alone.

Pen A Prayer

_____
_____
_____
_____
_____
_____
_____
_____

Jeremiah 1:1-8

Deliver

God is with me;
there is no
need to fear.

When I'm
experiencing
loneliness, what
promise from this
passage would refocus
my feelings?

_____
_____
_____
_____
_____
_____
_____
_____
_____

Praying the Promise

Dear God,

Thank you for being _____.

Please forgive me for _____.

Help me to recognize_____.

Your Word says _____

and I believe it. Please give me _____.

Show me how to _____.

I praise You for the victory.

Amen.

When I begin to feel lonely, I will pray God's promises in one of the following ways:
(Check your focus.)

- o Thank God that He is always with me.
- o Tell Him I believe that He is listening.
- o Ask God to help me notice His grace in my daily life.
- o Request the wisdom to see opportunities to embrace relationship.

Pen A Prayer

_____

_____

_____

_____

_____

_____

_____

_____

Declare

God is
with
me to
deliver me.

What is one
statement of truth
from this passage that
reminds me I'm not
alone?

_____
_____
_____
_____
_____
_____
_____
_____
_____

Praying the Promise

Dear God,

Thank you for being _____.

Please forgive me for _____.

Help me to recognize_____.

Your Word says _____

and I believe it. Please give me _____.

Show me how to _____.

I praise You for the victory.

Amen.

When I begin to feel lonely, I will pray God's promises in one of the following ways:
(Check your focus.)

- ○ Thank God that He will never leave me.
- ○ Tell Hm that I want to sense His presence.
- ○ Invite Him to encourage my heart to share His love.
- ○ Ask the Lord to help me see that I am not alone.

Pen A Prayer

_____

_____

_____

_____

_____

_____

_____

_____

_____

Victory

God goes with
me, to fight
for me against
the enemy.

When I'm
experiencing
loneliness, what
promise from this
passage would refocus
my feelings?

_____

_____

_____

_____

_____

_____

_____

_____

_____

Praying the Promise

Dear God,

Thank you for being _____.

Please forgive me for _____.

Help me to recognize_____.

Your Word says _____

and I believe it. Please give me _____.

Show me how to _____.

I praise You for the victory.

Amen.

When I begin to feel lonely, I will pray God's promises in one of the following ways:
(Check your focus.)

- ○ Thank God that He is always with me.
- ○ Tell Him I believe that He is listening.
- ○ Ask God to help me notice His grace in my daily life.
- ○ Request the wisdom to see opportunities to embrace relationship.

Pen A Prayer

_____

_____

_____

_____

_____

_____

_____

_____

Today's Battle Plan

1. Believe that God is with me.

2. Trust that He is FOR me.

3. Identify my true enemy.

4. Celebrate knowing God will provide the victory!

Psalm 36:1-12

Embrace

In His light,
I should see light
at the end of the
tunnel!

When I'm
experiencing
loneliness, what
promise from this
passage would refocus
my feelings?

_____
_____
_____
_____
_____
_____
_____
_____
_____

Praying the Promise

Dear God,
Thank you for being _____.
Please forgive me for _____.
Help me to recognize_____.
Your Word says _____
and I believe it. Please give me _____.
Show me how to _____.
I praise You for the victory.
Amen.

When I begin to feel lonely, I will pray God's promises in one of the following ways:
(Check your focus.)

o   Thank God that He will never leave me.
o   Tell Hm that I want to sense His presence.
o   Invite Him to encourage my heart to share His love.
o   Ask the Lord to help me see that I am not alone.

Pen A Prayer

_____

_____

_____

_____

_____

_____

_____

_____

Redeemed

The presence of the Lord provides peace, even in the most difficult times.

What is one statement of truth from this passage that reminds me I'm not alone?

_____
_____
_____
_____
_____
_____
_____
_____
_____

Praying the Promise

Dear God,

Thank you for being _____.

Please forgive me for _____.

Help me to recognize_____.

Your Word says _____

and I believe it. Please give me _____.

Show me how to _____.

I praise You for the victory.

Amen.

When I begin to feel lonely, I will pray God's promises in one of the following ways:
(Check your focus.)

o   Thank God that He is always with me.
o   Tell Him I believe that He is listening.
o   Ask God to help me notice His grace in my daily life.
o   Request the wisdom to see opportunities to embrace relationship.

Pen A Prayer

_____
_____
_____
_____
_____
_____
_____
_____
_____

Sometimes the boldest thing
we can do
is just take the next breath.
One More Step

Open

Jesus, reveal
your work
to me.

What is one
statement of truth
from this passage that
reminds me I'm not
alone?

_____
_____
_____
_____
_____
_____
_____
_____
_____

Praying the Promise

Dear God,

Thank you for being _____.

Please forgive me for _____.

Help me to recognize_____.

Your Word says _____

and I believe it. Please give me _____.

Show me how to _____.

I praise You for the victory.

Amen.

When I begin to feel lonely, I will pray God's promises in one of the following ways:
(Check your focus.)

- o Thank God that He will never leave me.
- o Tell Hm that I want to sense His presence.
- o Invite Him to encourage my heart to share His love.
- o Ask the Lord to help me see that I am not alone.

Pen A Prayer

_____

_____

_____

_____

_____

_____

_____

_____

Near

God is my refuge
and strength, a
very present help
in trouble.

When I'm
experiencing
loneliness, what
promise from this
passage would refocus
my feelings?

_____
_____
_____
_____
_____
_____
_____
_____
_____

Praying the Promise

Dear God,

Thank you for being _____.

Please forgive me for _____.

Help me to recognize_____.

Your Word says _____

and I believe it. Please give me _____.

Show me how to _____.

I praise You for the victory.

Amen.

When I begin to feel lonely, I will pray God's promises in one of the following ways:
(Check your focus.)

- ○ Thank God that He is always with me.
- ○ Tell Him I believe that He is listening.
- ○ Ask God to help me notice His grace in my daily life.
- ○ Request the wisdom to see opportunities to embrace relationship.

Pen A Prayer

_____

_____

_____

_____

_____

_____

_____

_____

Confidence

God's promises
fuel my
confidence to
move forward in
his work.

When I'm
experiencing
loneliness, what
promise from this
passage would refocus
my feelings?

_____
_____
_____
_____
_____
_____
_____
_____
_____

Praying the Promise

Dear God,

Thank you for being _____.

Please forgive me for _____.

Help me to recognize_____.

Your Word says _____

and I believe it. Please give me _____.

Show me how to _____.

I praise You for the victory.

Amen.

When I begin to feel lonely, I will pray God's promises in one of the following ways:
(Check your focus.)

○ Thank God that He will never leave me.
○ Tell Hm that I want to sense His presence.
○ Invite Him to encourage my heart to share His love.
○ Ask the Lord to help me see that I am not alone.

Pen A Prayer

_____

_____

_____

_____

_____

_____

_____

_____

Heart

God rules and reigns the heavens, yet he lives within my heart.

What is one statement of truth from this passage that reminds me I'm not alone?

_____
_____
_____
_____
_____
_____
_____
_____
_____

Praying the Promise

Dear God,

Thank you for being _____.

Please forgive me for _____.

Help me to recognize_____.

Your Word says _____

and I believe it. Please give me _____.

Show me how to _____.

I praise You for the victory.

Amen.

When I begin to feel lonely, I will pray God's promises in one of the following ways:
(Check your focus.)

- o Thank God that He is always with me.
- o Tell Him I believe that He is listening.
- o Ask God to help me notice His grace in my daily life.
- o Request the wisdom to see opportunities to embrace relationship.

Pen A Prayer

_____

_____

_____

_____

_____

_____

_____

_____

I serve a risen Savior
He's in the world today.
I know that He is living,
Whatever men may say.
I see His hand of mercy;
I hear His voice of cheer;
And just the time I need Him
He's always near.
He lives, He lives, Christ Jesus lives
today!
He walks with me and talks with me along
life's narrow way.
He lives, He lives, salvation to impart!
You ask me how I know He lives?
He lives within my heart.
Hymn, He Lives, Lyrics & Music Alfred Henry
Ackley, Public Domain

1 Kings 8:54-61

Day 26

With me

God was with me in the past, and will continue to be with me in the future.

When I'm experiencing loneliness, what promise from this passage would refocus my feelings?

_____
_____
_____
_____
_____
_____
_____
_____

Praying the Promise

Dear God,

Thank you for being _____.

Please forgive me for _____.

Help me to recognize_____.

Your Word says _____

and I believe it. Please give me _____.

Show me how to _____.

I praise You for the victory.

Amen.

When I begin to feel lonely, I will pray God's promises in one of the following ways:
(Check your focus.)

- o Thank God that He will never leave me.
- o Tell Hm that I want to sense His presence.
- o Invite Him to encourage my heart to share His love.
- o Ask the Lord to help me see that I am not alone.

Pen A Prayer

_____

_____

_____

_____

_____

_____

_____

_____

Steady

No matter what comes my way, I will not be shaken.

When I'm experiencing loneliness, what promise from this passage would refocus my feelings?

_____
_____
_____
_____
_____
_____
_____
_____
_____

Praying the Promise

Dear God,

Thank you for being _____.

Please forgive me for _____.

Help me to recognize_____.

Your Word says _____

and I believe it. Please give me _____.

Show me how to _____.

I praise You for the victory.

Amen.

When I begin to feel lonely, I will pray God's promises in one of the following ways:
(Check your focus.)

- o Thank God that He is always with me.
- o Tell Him I believe that He is listening.
- o Ask God to help me notice His grace in my daily life.
- o Request the wisdom to see opportunities to embrace relationship.

Pen A Prayer

_____

_____

_____

_____

_____

_____

_____

_____

Zeph. 3:14-20

God is on
every side of me.

What is one
statement of truth
from this passage that
reminds me I'm not
alone?

_____
_____
_____
_____
_____
_____
_____
_____

Praying the Promise

Dear God,

Thank you for being _____.

Please forgive me for _____.

Help me to recognize_____.

Your Word says _____

and I believe it. Please give me _____.

Show me how to _____.

I praise You for the victory.

Amen.

When I begin to feel lonely, I will pray God's promises in one of the following ways:
(Check your focus.)

o   Thank God that He will never leave me.
o   Tell Hm that I want to sense His presence.
o   Invite Him to encourage my heart to share His love.
o   Ask the Lord to help me see that I am not alone.

Pen A Prayer

_____

_____

_____

_____

_____

_____

_____

_____

1 John 3:18-24

When I abide, the Lord's presence is much sweeter and more real to my heart.

What is one statement of truth from this passage that reminds me I'm not alone?

_____
_____
_____
_____
_____
_____
_____
_____
_____

Praying the Promise

Dear God,

Thank you for being _____.

Please forgive me for _____.

Help me to recognize_____.

Your Word says _____

and I believe it. Please give me _____.

Show me how to _____.

I praise You for the victory.

Amen.

When I begin to feel lonely, I will pray God's promises in one of the following ways:
(Check your focus.)

- o Thank God that He is always with me.
- o Tell Him I believe that He is listening.
- o Ask God to help me notice His grace in my daily life.
- o Request the wisdom to see opportunities to embrace relationship.

Pen A Prayer

_____

_____

_____

_____

_____

_____

_____

_____

Abide.
To stay with,
continue,
remain in or
close to.

How near to
Jesus
do I really want
to be?

Psalm 72:12-20

Reassurance

God alone does
wondrous
things.

What is one
statement of truth
from this passage that
reminds me I'm not
alone?

_____
_____
_____
_____
_____
_____
_____
_____

Praying the Promise

Dear God,

Thank you for being _____.

Please forgive me for _____.

Help me to recognize_____.

Your Word says _____

and I believe it. Please give me _____.

Show me how to _____.

I praise You for the victory.

Amen.

When I begin to feel lonely, I will pray God's promises in one of the following ways:
(Check your focus.)

- ○ Thank God that He will never leave me.
- ○ Tell Hm that I want to sense His presence.
- ○ Invite Him to encourage my heart to share His love.
- ○ Ask the Lord to help me see that I am not alone.

Pen A Prayer

_____

_____

_____

_____

_____

_____

_____

_____

Psalm 27:1-10

Receive

My God always
opens his arms
for me.

What is one
statement of truth
from this passage that
reminds me I'm not
alone?

_____
_____
_____
_____
_____
_____
_____
_____
_____

Praying the Promise

Dear God,

Thank you for being _____.

Please forgive me for _____.

Help me to recognize_____.

Your Word says _____

and I believe it. Please give me _____.

Show me how to _____.

I praise You for the victory.

Amen.

When I begin to feel lonely, I will pray God's promises in one of the following ways:
(Check your focus.)

- o Thank God that He is always with me.
- o Tell Him I believe that He is listening.
- o Ask God to help me notice His grace in my daily life.
- o Request the wisdom to see opportunities to embrace relationship.

Pen A Prayer

_____

_____

_____

_____

_____

_____

_____

_____

Put a Bow on It!

You did it! You read your Bible for 31 days in a row!

Throughout this month of Scripture reading, I've been reminded God is always with me, Jesus sent the Holy Spirit to be with me, and he not only is with me, but lives in and through me!

We have the privilege to walk with Jesus each step of our days, recognizing his voice and embracing his presence, because he is with us.

I pray that as you've walked this 31-day path, you've enjoyed learning to look for God's work and enjoy his presence more intimately.

Thanks for joining me on this journey through the Bible. Discover more Bible reading plans & journals at http://rachelwojo.com/shop.

Additional Notes

About the Author

Rachel "Wojo" Wojnarowski is wife to Matt and mom to seven wonderful kids. Her greatest passion is inspiring others to welcome Jesus into their lives and enjoy the abundant life he offers.

As a sought-after blogger and writer, she sees thousands of readers visit her blog daily. Rachel leads community ladies' Bible studies in central Ohio and serves as an event planner and speaker. In her "free time" she crochets, knits, and sews handmade clothing. Okay, not really. She enjoys running and she's a tech geek at heart.

Reader, writer, speaker, and dreamer, Rachel can be found on her website at **RachelWojo.com.**

Free Bible Study Video Series

If you enjoyed this Bible reading plan & journal, then you'll love Rachel's free video Bible study to help you find strength for difficult seasons of life! **http://rachelwojo.com/free-bible-study-video-series-for-one-more-step/**

Feel like giving up?

Are you ready to quit? Give up? But deep down, you want to figure out how to keep on keeping on?

Like you, Rachel has faced experiences that crushed her dreams of the perfect life: a failed marriage, a daughter's heartbreaking diagnosis, and more. In this book, she transparently shares her pain and empathizes with yours, then points you to the path of God's Word, where you'll find hope to carry you forward. One More Step gives you permission to ache freely—and helps you believe that life won't always be this hard. No matter the circumstances you face, through these pages you'll learn to...

- persevere through out-of-control circumstances and gain a more intimate relationship with Jesus
- run to God's Word when discouragement strikes
- replace feelings of despair with truths of Scripture

If you enjoyed this Bible reading plan and journal, then you'll love:

http://rachelwojo.com/shop

Made in the
USA
Monee, IL